SURGE

SURGE

Etel Adnan

Nightboat Books
New York

Printed in the United States
Third Printing, 2024

ISBN: 978-1-937-65885-4

Design and typesetting by Kit Schluter
Text set in Italian Old Style MT

Cataloging-in-publication data is available
From the Library of Congress

Nightboat Books
New York
www.nightboat.org

for Denise Newman

Rains return to the sound of their origins when night begins to spread; over the land the night is as long as a city's deserted avenues,

… or the way to distant galaxies. The animals feel the disorientation.

Thoughts are metallic and melt in salt water. Their frequency increases the melancholy, the pervading melancholy.

Meaning is ephemeral.

The world reverberates its disorder, creates waves of determination.

A lit candle can bring out the whole absurdity of victories.

To look at the stones, out there, the cracked wall, the rain.

When a child, I was found in a basket, they said, full of roses, and with ribbons too. No thorns were mentioned.

*

Much has to do with what we mean by reality: is a basket's reality a concept, or a tool for keeping our feet grounded? (physically and mentally).

And was the basket as evident as the child?

We have a few certitudes to lay our shoulders on, and still we go on opening the shutters, welcoming friends ... in cities left-over by wars ...

People breathe heavily between the old nightmare and the dullness of the day. A simple question can raise reality's temperature.

The moon is more than I am, but she can't give more than what she is.

The heat and the cold fill many gaps, but is reality real? For now, the November sky is watery, California skies over artichoke fields, redwoods, trucks going south in the night.

Eleni sprang off her chair, raising her voice: "there's no reality any more!" That brought beauty to her eyes.

The fish's ability to shift environments makes me want to inhabit the tummy of any whale that swims by the coast, to get out of my skin and lie under his, on the first new moon of the year ...

and daydream for hours and hours.

*

How to dismiss century-old plane trees? They're murmuring during their spring renewal, in this Holy Week that tells me that I won't resurrect, not the way they do ...

Paradise is certainly a bore, unless it's still a garden. Solitude doesn't make for better thinking. Unfortunately. It can thicken the air, yes, it can do that.

Coming close to the sun, there's fear, tremendous fear.

Let's keep windows open to ease the anguish that the furniture exudes. The sea throws its waves very high. Salt for the Earth.

Oh to enter reality like a boat does the night!

Comprehensibility has nothing to do with the real.

Napoleon was indeed the Spirit of the World, as Hegel had wanted him to be, of its ever youthful violence, and mega-weapons followed, and dying lost meaning.

We witness night as the result of the high-jacking of light, a home for despair. A thousand souls in one body, in one soul ... body and soul dying at different times, different speeds.

"Time gives only what it has, and it has only what it is itself" —H.

Taking trains is soothing: Their steady rhythm penetrates the landscapes they traverse, trains and landscapes joining their wills, while many refugees living at the periphery of wars carry that rhythm in their veins.

*

But to arrive in a city is another story: it means running into commanders-in-chief who have mowed down entire villages, I mean just recently.

Even a mild earthquake can reduce one's self-confidence to shreds, but who dares question destiny? Tolstoi's peasants never did. Destiny was just a vaporous substance hovering over their bending backs, as Tolstoï was telling.

The light fades over my years and theaters close. With its sense of reality narrowed to a thread, my mind wanders beyond the twenty-four hours of the day. There isn't much I can do.

A river-bed on Mars white-dotted craters a moving video that's all.

Is death by water a baptism? In my inner territory my spirit flies very low, next to helicopters, at their level. There's nothing to grasp in there; in its lowlands, there's not a way to shore up one's will. I shelter a swamp.

The summer fog whose recurring walls, seen from the north of the Bay, obliterate San Francisco regularly ... is turning the city into a ghost town. Is San Francisco hallucinating?

Is fog a sheen over clouds that are tired and collapsed, lifeless? But it keeps me as spellbound as a sailor nearing the mists of the Equator. Yes, it recreates my spirit.

Snow is for the winter. Usually.

*

Strangely, what was a fluffy reality a few hours ago becomes a soft, long, all encompassing silvery river, its lightness moves on.

Now, there's a surrender to the sea even though some energy is inadvertently left. There are no storms over the sinkholes, but tides, yes, immense tides, that never hurry.

I swim in "night" the largest of all oceans.

I hear sirens, see ducks sliding on the water's surface; deep reflections. The water follows the ducks with no breaks. It's hearts that get broken, not waters, not rivers.

Sounds silence ordinary language, put it to sleep. Music is the vibration of time itself in an uninterrupted surge, the modulation of thinking, the moon's hidden side, making time inevitable.

Peter Gizzi's broad smile is worth a thousand stories.

I hear that close to Arabia's western coast a range of mountains are regularly getting ready for a voyage east. At the other end, people are waiting and waiting ...

We're not dealing with a mirage but with something foreign to our understanding. And the sun leaps over the earth and leaves behind shadows so numerous that they can be picked up with one's hand.

Then the shadows float down softly, the air trembles. The air trembles.

Let the sea enter!

Nobody knows where from life springs, but it does, like reality from a Heidegger book. Normally, I see a rug on the floor, chairs, probably a dog, and it's easy. And probably all wrong.

Remembering the Greeks: Being at its fullness when appearing, the presence of a simple pebble transcending.

Being appears, and withdraws. In Nietzsche's view, it returns.

Anyway, I don't "see" ideas, should I? The eyeglasses on my brain need a replacement, though I wonder if they are altogether indispensable. Can we move without being aware of distance?

In the early hours of the day, fishermen on the way home create in us the sense of their presence, but we may as well be facing just their shape, a wholeness not different from emptiness. The suspension of definitions.

*

And many hours later all that's left are the scintillating waters of the ocean, moving surfaces running into the horizon, the sinking of color into light!

Where are the old debates, the old dust? Sufis used to travel from Murcia to Cairo—up through the airs—using for fuel the power of their will (if birds can do it, why not them?) The real must have meant the miles they covered, and only that. With, underneath, the grounds shaking.

Awareness is always of the past. Sailing.

The ocean is wetter today, winds and clouds are busy.

My inner screen is visited by Mexico, but I may be facing a pure creation. But whose creation? Mine? Not really. It's rather the surging in my brain of an event, magnetic and immaterial, taking the form of the name of that country.

Then, how can this inner and cloudy stirring, not defined and still present, just a word, be Mexico, or have anything to do with it?

The sound of that word seems to come out of nowhere: does it mean places I had visited, sites I wish I had gone to? In what mess am I swimming?

When I recall, let's say, my mother, am I having a new look at her, or do I see repeatedly a fixed image of her, forever the same?

*

It can well be that Empedocles threw himself into the Popocatépetl (and not in his Sicilian volcano). Nobody on record witnessed the moment.

Probably not Empedocles himself, as I doubt he could have watched his own death, at least not what happened after his last breath.

Nostalgia is a secret, since it's out of fashion, a secret. What would happen if hordes of angels visited us, will we then enter their zone, share their ways, become who they are? (wings included!) Do we love Empedocles?

... I, for one, will look for him, still...but where?

While thinking of him I listen to the hum of the river that rushes down my piece of land. That's what I do.

I also hear the air flowing with it, its unbroken surface leading one's imagination to more water, more destabilization, more wind.

And from the tides, what's left? The fact that we're rhythms and to each his own, that they don't merge with anything alien, that they can't be trespassed, and so on.

The moon—to whom the night is still entrusted—is regularly receding into its own shadow, into the past. My life has been disappearing along its wanderings, though I'm surrounded by an abundance of life, and the inaccessibility of the future ...

its sister planet is not listening.

We're past-ing uninterruptedly. Better be confined in a submarine's opacity, be numbed. And love, always in the future tense, also past-ing, meant to collapse, a draft of air, air filling the world.

So we speak of the pitiful state of the Earth, then, once at home, light the computer, let our fear of the void project itself with a force that has no materiality. Oh the computer that replaces the cinema of the lost years!

Reality is made of paper, so to speak, or is the skin of an egg, an onion to be peeled, till you reach another layer, itself made of layers, with no center, you also reach a mirror mirroring, a sailboat drifting.

Your identity is your prison.

The real has no use for any metaphysical grounding. Everything is shifty, above all the products of the brain. The mind acts as a revolving lamp that projects itself on itself too, and on this and that ...

This chair, facing me, wants to get out from this world, but the world keeps expanding.

*

Death exists only for the others. Then, tell me, can we keep speaking of the dead as we do of people alive?

It's time for the birds to take off. The night has indeed been long. This Saturday morning pictures of Tomales Bay taken from Bolinas Ridge are being projected on the net. They come from a region that's home, now as far away as these birds would fly to.

These will go where I won't. It's terrifying to feel that all the places I long for will remain forbidden, remain virtual, and still will haunt me.

Bolinas has been framed and hung. It was burning with heat when Brautigan splashed his brain on one of its walls—and when Duncan McNaughton was thinking: "We are full in California of dreams gone." From mind we usually return to mind.

Thinking calls for more thinking, in mazes of abstractions, oblivious of whatever is apprehended as an instant, while belonging to time's eternity. But isn't reality as Eugénie Paultre said, the tissue of time: "la réalité est la matière du temps."

In perception, redemption.

I was chased by a snowstorm, still shivering, couldn't see nor hear; not having a shadow, but the world was moving with me, we were twins.

*

God must be the theologian of the void, as we learned that creation sprang out of a nothingness that was prior to it. We may also be speaking nonsense. But that's pretty hard to admit.

Babylonians said that deities created man from clay mixed with the blood of a slain god. They acknowledged the divine in us.

Let's be on solid ground: the universe is. Its is-ness is its definition and History is the biography of Being.

Mountains rise in us, as language does, making of analogy an intrinsic part of thinking (therefore, of being).

So mountains are languages and languages are mountains.

We speak both.

The fire licked its way up. A line of bison crossed the land, and over there a camel-driver found his way.

All this was ominous, but still was of no importance compared to the spirit, the spirit which is at its best when empty.

I don't want to be sending farewells to an ordinary world, a world, by the way, wounded beyond repair.

But recently, objects started to scare me, as they seem to be aware of their independence, and, pushing their arrogance further, are having their own meditations interfere with mine.

*

The bells of revenge are tolling: a spirit must be inhabiting these so-called inanimate things—that our theologies have despised for so long—as we have to deal with countless kinds of spirits, each with an assigned residence.

Waves keep coming but the sea doesn't move, and sunrises are parallel to sunsets.

Clouds of dust are filling the sky from end to end. We're out of sync with words. They remind us of atoms as they fuse their parts to create continuity, words making thoughts, particles making matter ... where's the difference? Let's leave reality deal with itself.

Every time I say "I know" I must be meaning "I am" (that simple?!). I keep repeating I am night, a statement as treacherous as the seasons, as unpredictable as they are, sensitive to humidity, improbable.

If you want to rest from the moon's haunting power, take a pencil and write on paper: "moon", then stop. That's what Bob Grenier does. Some follow the trajectory of a ball in a ball game. Others see the hand of God on a gun's trigger. Poets remain the keeper of language, for whatever it's worth.

What about the painters? They "keep" nothing. They gather for drinks, for many drinks, after a day's work; their kind of a language has yet to be decoded.

Birds fly, and leave no traces.

Nothing ever rests, least of all this engine we call the brain, with its continuous soft nuclear eruption that we call the mind. But the stomach contains more neurons that this brain we hold in such awe; we mistreat this repository of food until we find some cures for its illnesses.

I am probably a "rainy" night, thick and soft, en route to encounter Paul Klee's (or his phantom's) stride over the land, and Roger Snell's letters, (and pebbles, the asphalt, wandering nymphs, remembrances of cold, frozen fields).

During a darkest night I did away with the word "I" on my way to being just a being. The land was of the past. We will soon return to inhabiting trees (if any are left).

It's alright; the earth's crust is incredibly thin and the fire underneath erupts as volcanoes. Did Empedocles ever water his rosebushes? If he had done so he would have lived longer, how to know?

This pure moment: light over light.

Space expanding, getting out of the way.

*

Silence in free fall. And water watering itself.

Further away light eating at light annihilating itself in greater intensity, entering the infinite.

Flowers are as obsolete as people. If you had to choose between the Mississippi and your neighbor wouldn't you rather vote for the grand river's survival? I would.

The city is sinking in repression. In front of the church of Saint Sulpice there's a huge poster advertising the perfect family: a little boy, his father, and a robot. Did the robot replace the mother, or is he (or it) considered the ideal playmate for the child?

The feeling of a subtle and imminent apocalypse is taking hold of the place, in contrast to the flowing waters of the fountain that enchant the area.

In the church, Delacroix's angels feel that they would need to return to paradise to warn their legions that a new Faust is born, as the old Faust has been revised, then murdered.

They already see that the robot that's arrogantly standing on the wall, in open air, will grow and multiply, that old ladies, worn down by their loneliness, will soon, by the millions, fall desperately in love with him. The angels will cry.

*

Oh, to come down from Dante's Paradise and end up spending afternoons with these creatures whose skulls are made of steel, and eyes of glass!

Bells are ringing, farmers are out on the streets. The beach will linger on the perimeter of one's sleep.

In sleep, lands.

Labyrinths reach for open air—the open fields of southern Greece.

It's essential not to lose one's mind, even knowing that minds come cheap, inflation affecting them too; every head one sees in the street is carrying (at least) one.

The real requires patience. "The love that moves the sun and other stars" never wears a mask: It's available. It's generous, too. And let's be as resilient as it is.

We keep wondering about the mind's resting place, in relation to reality. How do they manage to put up with each other? Mind is not reason, not an entity. It covers matter as moisture will do. It functions smoothly one day, then drifts ...

Sometimes mind becomes submissive. If it were an energy it would have had an origin, but does it have one? It's not spatial, but it is the one to say so. We focus it on ideas, on itself too. To gain what? And who is this "we"?

*

The universe may end as sheer light ... the light might not end.

I am the tide that incessantly moves, and we incessantly part away.

Mind can be gone; how to figure out where and why?!
In the here and now, we're mulling over the slaughter
of Moby Dick in the cold waters of the Arctic by
Japanese killer-gangs, fishermen-daemons.

In the world at large there will be no attention paid
to this archetypal aquatic hero, no burial. His death
is the terminal episode of a confrontation that pitted
the American nation against the rest of the world for
more than a couple of centuries.

This time he has been killed not by Ahab, the father,
but for a pitiful amount of money.

Saying this, all there's left on the scene is the policeman
over there, watching.

Mount Fuji surged during a summer night and Earth
made room for it.

Poets resist the worship of death. Death is powerful,
all too-powerful, but it's death, so we shouldn't even

give it a name. But we feel too well this surging of a fear in the obscurity of the organs, this obscurity, this incestuous pain.

*

Yellow leaves in yellow wind.

The religion of the Chinese is their history, pretty soon, our own.

We pretend to imagine a galaxy, we're crazy, after all. The cosmos wants to retire, why not? Hale and thunder are its voice on this side of its beauty. We hold onto anything that comes by: a twig, a sound.

As we're always living in prehistory, the future will never happen.

Where, and why, make good questions when the fog covers our space totally or a marriage goes wrong. Wondering over such matters gets us nowhere, but to live is also to think.

We can't stop this inner flow, this river of ideas that traverses our brain, that we freeze, and call it mind, call it the bed of reality.

There's a sweetness to existence, a saying renewed, shadows that bring rest, the attenuation of angles, the growth of plants ...

The trees by the edge of the terrace carry on their tops my desire to soar, but I am made of

fluids. And I need friends. I would have in this very moment gone fly-fishing with Russell Chatham, though it had to happen sooner.

The voyage to the sun is a voyage into the past.

After his long trips into California's wilderness, rafting and climbing, Russell always came home to his desk and writing, his studio and painting. I see the silence that surrounds him like the sky does his canvases. In love's deepest sense.

This morning the fog entered the door, crossed the room, then went straight out the window. Me, observing for a lifetime this very event. Absurdity happens daily.

Standing by the Pacific Ocean. The ocean.

Paradise has rivers, it has been said. I think that it's a dry country with only mountains.

Madness can run as a sweat over the brain (and on the rest of the body) and evaporate from the line of one's head.

We live in days when we mistreat Nature, and keep asking her to come to our rescue.

It's given, then taken away.

*

At some point, we'll stand, move, go, will not return.

Time continues to speed frantically, remembering that it was once a divinity. It knew then, at least, what it was.

We pretend to measure the invisible and the unknown. It can all be just some entertainment. Better to claim ignorance, with pride, (we need the pride of not-knowing, the breathing space).

Some weight has fallen over my house, (it spared the apple trees of the garden). In the interval, many thoughts expressed in many languages have piled up.

Thinking takes time, and probably resembles time, as we can't figure out what each is, or how they interact, or view themselves.

The tide comes at its own pace; this is why it never commits a crime.

Reality started to flow in the courtyard we name the real; we have no idea how the transformation came to be, or where in hot days the water is going—Philosophy used to deal with such things, but it ended in bankruptcy, like downtown, the banks.

Let the dead bury the dead; that's what we told a man who had just lost a son to a car accident. In the harbor, lines of boats—as bouncy as ever—are getting ready to go, to start a voyage out, and the place is resonating with voices.

Between the will and its destination there might be fields and fields. But the will can bend and not recede. I still prefer love's power, though it keeps us dangling between obscurity and daylight.

Love is the result of a throw of dice, Mallarmé's historic throw. Sometimes it surges with the evidence of a theorem in geometry, cleans out everything on its way —lands us on a remote planet, yet, it can sink in a gutter, kicking fallen leaves down the side of a dirt road ...

A radical pain traversed my life from end to end—a large band of light crossed the moon's hidden face. That kind of motion alters the world.

"Not all days are ripe for keeping"
Yes, Tom, they're not.

We said that predicting something may bring about its end; so I will suspend judgment. Anyway, our financial systems are weaving around our necks a network of steel in which we're entangled slowly and surely ...

*

Spiders crawling over the beds. How long can we endure the wretched forms that misery is taking? Killing fields are daily bread.

Then let everything go to hell! The proliferation of the circles of anxiety slows down the imagination. (But don't worry, you can still not care).

But what's this 'something' that we call the imagination? Let's see. There's the will, on one hand, intelligence on the other. Imagination must therefore be the vehicle that brings the one to the other, another way to say that it connects us to the world; or, to put it differently, brings order to what would have been viewed as natural chaos.

Imagination alleviates terror, creating both the windows and what we see. It gives power to the mind — if by mind we name the fusion of will, intellect and imagination.

It is true that the mind splits itself in order not to be just in touch with itself, but to move ahead and attend other businesses. It was said that the imagination is the intermediary between us and the platonic ideas.

(only under clear skies?)

It was also said that it is the stairway, so to speak, that led some mystics—

and some fools—closest to the divine. All that can be true—according, precisely, to one's imagination.

We have also to think of it as being a mercurial element that interprets memories, makes them evident. It can also wreck the ship.

Images don't come from the imagination. They grow like weeds from the fields of the invisible.

Memory belongs to cosmic forces, acts with the unpredictability of those horses that stun crowds and win races. We share it, we do not own it; when deprived of it we remain speechless, dumb.

We are such that in us memory needs another facet of itself, ultimately that other energy that we call the real. Otherwise, it would be useless and wouldn't that energy help the renewal of forests, I wonder.

The real addresses itself to our senses, as they are tuned to it. Memory "holds" the real in sight, gives it depth; with the help of the imagination, its friend, it shapes the real, makes it appear in a variety of forms without which reality itself—the master concept sustaining the whole edifice—would vanish.

*

In that sense we can admit that we "make" the real "appear," although it is here, on its own right, with its own power, we being its visitors ... We are born to the real, and dying is a parting away, a separation, the last way of telling it good-bye.

We have to say yes to that fate, and it's hard, the hardest.

We're naked entering, and naked we leave.

But the world, while we're still around, is mother, and child, an orchard crumbling under its own flowers, giving us the means to be, while resulting from our own doing ... an on-going apparition.

The real is home. Assuredly. And is also reverberating within reality.

Strangely — although we can't tame the real which seems so familiar, we in some ways are the ones to make reality, as angelic intellects, though that will remain mercurial, unstable at best.

We are running two beasts, impervious to the feasibility of the project ...

Joanne Kyger died a week ago, in Bolinas. Black energy claimed her body. Life is real, for sure, but it's perverse, and gives up on us. Then death intrudes, creates holes in the heart. Where is she? Hard to think that she's nowhere. She's here, if I can say, with us, lonelier, but where?

She had said that what we're used to calling life is death, and that death is the beginning of life, if we dare remember, and written this on January 20, 2010:

On the other side of the road
the huge surge of the ocean makes an enormous commotion
inside the commotion
the whole history of sea
every note it's ever made

At the crossroads
of fact and imagination
without overstatement
without fantasy

We're led to think that poetry is the space where an object and its other territory, or the real and reality, meet, in clearest evidence, for the real to move into reality, and reality be the real.

Conversations with my soul
(III)

My soul, you're close by,
not in me,
we ought to get together,
I miss you

I am night, I keep saying,
living in dark luminosity,

a rainy night

was 4 years old, and 5,
and more,
when swimming every summer

Grains of sand contain
secrets,
that can be deadly

I feed on memories
remember most
Hart Crane's coat on the
railing,
the wave's open mouth

The beach is endless,
the continent empty,
waiting for the soul's return

But where's my soul? —
only in the question

Long corridors appear
a voyage underground
hard tunnels

A few stamps, a pencil
what is close, is far away –
like a bridge

The East River advances in waves
like one's thinking,
to rather be the river

There's life in life,
death in death,
both accelerating

An ocean resides between my
eye and its eyelid

To chase the Pacific's horizons I
will need an infinity of lives

In a civilization of dispersion
to be autumn leaves

Dark national elections,
irreversible...

Clearly, nothing is clear

Color is a particular manifestation of light
everything else is doubtful

We live in imaginary countries

know that food will soon
be unavailable;
that the end will end

I caused pain,
overlooked her need for life

then we each went away

When I too will disappear
we will be lost
once more for ever

The sun has aged, weary for
dragging along
its turbulent planets

Transparency emerges when the time has
come to revive by any available window
a shred of reality

Nietzsche kissed a horse. He, at last, found
a friend. We're the ones to be
crying

A long night I spent
thinking that reality was the story
of the human species

the vanquished search for the vanquished

Sounds come by, ruffling my soul

I sense space's elasticity,
go on reading the books she wrote on the
wars she's seen

Why do seasons who regularly follow
their appointed time, deny their kind of energy
to us?

why is winter followed by a few
more days of winter?

We came to transmit the shimmering
from which we came; to name it

we deal with a permanent voyage,
the becoming of that which itself had
become

Night is a shadow due to interferences
with the sun's divine path,
a river running through its opposite

The principle of reality filters the real
which faints into it
the operation is epiphanic:
the surging, into an instant, of an instant

Reality is messianic   apocalyptic
my soul is my terror

Etel Adnan was born in Beirut, Lebanon in 1925. She studied philosophy at the Sorbonne, U.C. Berkeley, and at Harvard, and taught at Dominican College in San Rafael, California, from 1958-1972. In 1972, she returned to Beirut and worked as cultural editor for two daily newspapers. Her novel *Sitt Marie-Rose*, published in Paris in 1977, won the France-Pays Arabes award and has been translated into more than ten languages. In 1977, Adnan re-established herself in California, making Sausalito her home, with frequent stays in Paris. Etel Adnan died in Paris in 2021.

Adnan is the author of more than a dozen books in English, including *Journey to Mount Tamalpais* (1986); *The Arab Apocalypse* (1989); *In the Heart of the Heart of Another Country* (2005); *Sea and Fog* (2012), winner of the Lambda Literary Award for Lesbian Poetry and the California Book Award for Poetry; and *Night* (2016). *To look at the sea it to become what one is*, a two-volume collection of writing, was published in 2014, the same year she was awarded France's l'Ordre de Chevalier des Arts et Lettres. Her poems have been put to music by Tania Leon, Henry Treadgill, Gavin Bryars, Zad Moultaka, Annea Lockwood, and Bun Ching Lam. Exhibitions of her paintings have been mounted at The CCA Wattis Institute for Contemporary Arts, San Francisco; Museum der Moderne Salzburg; Mathaf: Arab Museum of Modern Art, Doha; and the Serpentine Galleries, London.

NIGHTBOAT BOOKS

Nightboat Books, a nonprofit organization, seeks to develop audiences for writers whose work resists convention and transcends boundaries. We publish books rich with poignancy, intelligence, and risk. Please visit nightboat.org to learn more about us and how you can support our future publications.

The following individuals have supported the publication of this book. We thank them for their generosity and commitment to the mission of Nightboat Books:

Elizabeth Motika
Benjamin Taylor

In addition, this book has been made possible, in part, by grants from the New York State Council on the Arts Literature Program and the Topanga Fund, which is dedicated to promoting the arts and literature of California.